Looking Good

LET'S PARTY

by Jacqueline A. Ball

Rourke Publications, Inc.
Vero Beach, FL 32964

Library of Congress Cataloging-in-Publication Data

Ball, Jacqueline A., 1952-
   Let's party! / by Jacqueline A. Ball.
      p.   cm. — (Looking good)
   Includes bibliographical references.
   Summary: Describes how to plan fabulous parties.
Includes recipes, instructions for making invitations and
decorations, and ideas for games and activities.
   1. Children's parties—Juvenile literature. 2. Entertaining-
Juvenile literature. [1. Parties. 2. Entertaining.] I. Title.
II. Series: Looking good (Vero Beach, Fla.)
GV1205.B35   1990   89-35899
793.2'1—dc 20   CIP
ISBN 0-86625-418-8   AC

CONTENTS

LET'S PARTY

When is a good time for a party? Some occasions seem tailor-made for parties: birthdays, graduations, Halloween. Think again; any time is a good time for good friends, good food, and good fun.

All parties can be fun, but some parties are truly fabulous. What makes the difference? Really special get-togethers—the ones people talk about and remember—take time, effort, a little money, but most of all, **planning**.

You may have decided it's party time, but it isn't up to just you alone. Now you need to have an important conversation with some important people: your parents. You need your parents' permission to have the party. Now is the time to get the ground rules straight. Pick a time to talk when both you and your parents are relaxed and not rushing off in a million directions.

Clear the date. To give yourself enough planning time, choose a date that's three or four weeks away. Make sure that the date is convenient for them. Most of all, make sure that at least one of them plans to be home. Why?

Any teenage party needs chaperones. You and your guests will be very glad adults are around if uninvited guests come crashing. Don't worry, most parents try to be as "invisible" as they can be during their teenagers' parties. They won't want to hang around and spoil your fun, but they'll want to be present.

TIP: Plan a party at a playground.
The clean-up can be done quickly
and easily.

Check out restrictions. Determine which rooms or places you can or cannot use. Can you count on the kitchen being yours for the whole night? Will you and your guests be allowed to dance, use the VCR, or exercise equipment? Where should people park their cars? These are just a few of the questions that should be asked. Don't assume you know what your parents will or won't let you do. It's always better to ask.

Once you know your parents' feelings on all these subjects, there's one last critical area that must be covered: you need to promise your folks that there won't be any alcohol or drugs at the party. Plan what to do if anyone does bring liquor or drugs that night.

This issue goes way beyond your family's rules or beliefs. It's a matter of law. It's illegal for anyone, regardless of age, to use certain drugs for recreational purposes. It's illegal for people under the age of twenty-one to drink in most states. You could get your parents and yourself into serious trouble if you don't obey these laws. Under certain circumstances, your parents could actually be arrested. Furthermore, there's always the risk of a tragic accident if someone tries to drive while under the influence.

Make the promise and stick to it. If the night of the party arrives and certain guests make things hard for you, well, that's why you have parents, and that's a big reason why they must be there that night. Antisocial behavior on the part of some guests may give you some real insight into who your friends really are.

How many people can you invite? At this point, you might not even know yourself how big a crowd you want, but see if your parents want to set a limit.

The mix of people is crucial. Don't invite people you know can't stand each other. Don't invite people who you know aren't good sports. Pick guests you know are fun-loving and will contribute to everyone's enjoyment of the evening.

Figuring out a good guest list might not be easy. Parties *are* people. The most delicious food, the most entertaining activities can't offset a bunch of obnoxious, rude, or boring guests. So choose carefully.

Get started by making an "ideal" guest list. Just write down the names of everyone you'd really like to invite. As you make up your list, keep these considerations in mind.

Who's invited you to a party lately? If you owe someone an invitation, remember your manners and repay it now.

Who would expect to be invited? Once the word gets out (and it will) that you're having a party, who will be hurt if left out? On the other hand, you're not obligated to invite someone you really dislike. As a general rule, however, if at all possible, include, don't exclude people.

Do you want to get to know someone better? Male or female, now is your chance!

All girls? All boys? Unless it's a sleepover, you'll probably want both. You should have the same number of each, but it's not absolutely critical.

How are you going to pay for this shindig? Parties take
money. Not necessarily a lot of money, but some. At your
age, you will probably be expected to pay all or a large part
of the expenses yourself. Now is the time to see if Mom
and Dad will supplement your party funds.

TIP: If you have a really good friend,
why not ask her to give the
party with you? You'll have twice
the creative ideas and half
the expense.

THE BIG FOUR

There are four elements that must be carefully thought out for a successful party: location, people, entertainment, and food.

Where's the Party?

Let's talk about the place first. Exactly where are you going to put all those party animals? In some ways, the place is the least important of the "Big Four," because if you have the other three you can throw a wonderful party virtually anywhere. Even so, with decorations, lighting, and furniture arrangement, you can give a place such a flavor or feeling that it just *makes* the party. You can create environments that are cozy and romantic, upbeat and lively, or eerie and ghostlike—and without spending a fortune either.

A great place for a party is a garage. If it's heated, you could even consider a sleepover there. Garages are usually big enough to accommodate a lot of people, and your family probably won't be too fussy about spills and spots, and wear and tear. You can decorate to your heart's content.

Having the party in the garage keeps the action out of the house, so the rest of the family doesn't have to hide out in their bedrooms all night. It keeps the noise at arm's length, too.

If you don't have a garage, or it can't be decorated to look right, how about the basement? It has most of the same advantages as the garage, except it's probably messier and more noise will carry into the house. It may even be bigger than the garage. The family room or living room are other choices, of course. For a sleepover, your own bedroom may be big enough. You probably can't handle more than eight people, unless you have tons of space and at least two bathrooms at your disposal.

For a regular indoor party, you should probably keep it to about twelve guests. More than that is a crowd. For outdoor parties, you'll probably be able to handle up to sixteen people comfortably.

You may want to have an outdoor party on the lawn, patio, or deck. (If that's the case, you'll probably want to get started in the afternoon, while it's still light.) Be prepared to move indoors in case of rain.

You might want all or part of the party to take place away from home entirely: at the movies, a pizza place, the bowling alley, or at a ball game. You'll have to work out transportation and make arrangements for tickets. You would be expected to pay for your guests, and that would certainly limit the number of people you can invite.

How much will you spend? Obviously, that depends on how much food you're going to serve, and what additional costs there might be. Figure on spending at least $3.00 per person, no matter how simple you keep it. That figure could climb as high as $6.00 or $7.00, or even more! Knowing these facts, you might need to eliminate some people from your ideal list, or you might want to change the nature of your party.

BUDGET

GUESTS

NAME	DATE	ANSWER
SALLY	10/1	yes
TOM	9/31	no
CINDY	10/2	yes
SUE	10/1	yes
JOEY	10/3	yes
SARAH	10/3	yes
JEANNIE	10/4	no

FOOD/DRINKS -

INVITATIONS -

EQUIPMENT -

DECORATIONS -

ENTERTAINMENT -

MISCELLANEOUS - TOTAL -

YOU ARE INVITED
to the HALLOWE'EN PARTY of
Lissa Mathews and Ashley Hall
OCTOBER 31st
7:00 to 11:00 P.M.
640 MAIN ST.
wear a costume
Prizes!
466-4431
RSVP
Name:
Yes I'm coming:
Sorry, I can't attend:

Invitations

Everyone loves to be invited somewhere, so you're about to make some people very happy. The simplest way to extend the invitation is by telephone. It's also the cheapest way. Telephoning is an especially good idea if everyone knows where you live and you don't have a lot of information to tell.

If there is a lot of information—directions, instructions, etc.— you're better off sending written invitations. Besides, written ones make the whole thing somehow more official, and they can be saved for souvenirs later.

You can buy packaged invitations at discount stores, card stores, department stores, and even at some super-markets—or you can make your own. You'll save money that way (although you'll still have to pay for stamps) and they'll be truly unique, giving invited guests a glimpse of how special your party is going to be.

One way to customize invitations is to cut them out of construction paper in shapes related to the theme of your party; witches' hats and bats for Halloween, a sombrero for a Mexican fiesta, hearts or a pair of lips for Valentine's Day. Then simply write the information on the shape in some contrasting color.

Or how about ghost-written invitations, if you want to be mysterious? Use plain white paper. At the top of the page, print in ink: Mystery Message: Hold over lighted lamp to read. Write the rest of the party information with a cotton swab dipped in lemon juice. This invisible ink will become readable when exposed to the warmth of the lamp or any source of direct heat.

You can make puzzling invitations by writing information on lightweight cardboard, trimming it with a pretty border, then cutting the board up into jigsaw puzzle pieces. Put the pieces in an envelope and mail. Guests will have to assemble the puzzle to get the scoop.

Another trick involves balloons. Blow up balloons and write the information on them with Magic Marker. Then deflate them. Place in envelopes and mail.

If you hand-carry your invitations, write them on long scrolls of paper with a thick-line black pen or marker. Roll them up and insert them into cardboard tubes saved from toilet tissue, waxed paper, etc. Cut the tubes if necessary. The tubes should be decorated. For a special touch, tie a ribbon around the scroll before inserting.

Here's one last idea: Baby Face. Get a baby picture of yourself (black and white works best). Make photocopies and paste them on the invitations. Ask guests to bring their own baby pictures and, at the party, mount them on a board. See if other guests can figure out who *was* who!

Get the invitations out as soon as possible. You want people to have plenty of notice so they won't already be booked up.

TIP: Don't issue invitations, verbal or written, at school. It can really cause hurt feelings among those who aren't asked.

Fun and Games

You want to keep your guests busy with lots of fun things to do all night. Don't assume that kids will spend their time talking to each other. Maybe they will, but you must be ready with some entertainment. If that night comes and everyone is having a wonderful time just chatting away, then you won't have to put your plans in motion. You can always *not* do something, but you *can't* always come up with something suddenly to save a boring party.

Just as is the case with food, you can be as plain or fancy as you want with the games, activities, and entertainment. Some popular activities are: board games such as Pictionary and Trivial Pursuit, dancing, watching videos, playing word games such as Mad-Libs or Scrabble. If outdoors, play softball, volleyball, or have a scavenger hunt.

> **TIP:** What will *this* particular collection of people, in *this* particular setting, be most comfortable doing? *That's* the key question.

Knowing your guests and being familiar with the space you have available are important factors in picking the entertainment. Not everyone is good at Trivial Pursuit, for instance, or at word games. People often have different tastes in videos, with some going in for the scariest, bloodiest horror movies and other preferring light comedy or romance. If you live in a remote area without many other houses nearby, a scavenger hunt is not a good idea, neither is a softball game if your backyard is tiny.

15

Food, Glorious Food

Now you know who's coming. Next question: What will you feed them? You want food that looks attractive and that people will eat eagerly. This is not the time for something exotic, or something like artichokes that people might not even know how to eat. You want tasty food, and lots of it.

You want beverages that aren't loaded with caffeine (to keep your guests from bouncing off walls). Avoid red fruit punches, and don't even think about grape juice. They'll stain.

You can keep the whole thing simple and just offer munchies: chips, pretzels, popcorn, and soda or punch. Add some cookies or a cake and everyone will be reasonably satisfied.

You can get a little fancier by adding something substantial like sandwiches. It's especially fun to build a giant ham or turkey grinder on crusty French bread, and then slice it into individual wedges. You can turn ordinary peanut butter and jelly or tuna fish sandwiches into something special by using cookie cutters to make pretty shapes.

Of course, takeout food is high on the list of easy party refreshments. You can order pizza, or Chinese food, or fried chicken, or hamburgers.

All of these alternatives are OK. They satisfy two big party food requirements: *they're not too messy*, and *they can be eaten standing up*. Most of them don't require any knives or forks. Finger food is the best party fare. Still, if you want your party to be *more* than OK, have your guests help you prepare part of the meal.

FIRST SHOPPING TRIP

It's never too early to start stocking up on party provisions. When you still have a few weeks to go, you can start buying items that will keep. First, of course, check with Mom or Dad to make sure there's a place to put them. Don't buy fresh fruit, vegetables, or dairy products. They won't keep. If you want, you can buy meat and bread and freeze it.

You first shopping list could include things such as:
- Cans or bottles of fruit juice
- Mustard, ketchup, tomato or spaghetti sauce
- Paper plates, napkins, plastic glasses
- Bottles of soda or sparkling water
- Tea
- Cake or cookie mixes or ingredients
- Balloons, crepe paper, or other decorating supplies
- Bags of chips or snacks

TIP: Check the expiration date on anything you buy.

Exactly what you purchase will depend on your menu, theme, and entertainment. Whatever your specific shopping needs, you can keep expenses down if you keep these thoughts in mind:

Beg or borrow first. Before you purchase anything, see if you can get it free any other way. You should spend money only if you must. For instance, you can ask your guests to bring their videos or board games. You can make ice yourself, freezing trays starting a week or so before the party. Mom might let you use the everyday china and silverware, so you won't need disposable items (thereby doing a favor to the environment as well as your wallet). Your own kitchen probably contains all the spices, herbs, and baking staples you need. Create your own decorations.

Buy the store brand. It will almost always be cheaper.

Buy the largest sized bottles of soda. Don't buy individual (12-ounce) cans or bottles. People won't finish them, so some of the beverage will be wasted or spilled, and all those cans create a disposal problem.

Buy large size bags of potato chips, pretzels, etc. To figure out how much beverage you'll need, figure that each guest will drink at least three 8-ounce glasses. For a slumber party, where the girls will be drinking (and eating) all night, figure on more. It's always better to have too much than not enough.

What about extras? Make sure there are enough hangers for coats. Every party needs music. Do you have tapes? Do you need batteries for your tape deck? Games? Film for the camera? Balloons? Light bulbs?

THE WEEKEND BEFORE

The days are flying by. Your party is fast approaching! By now you should: know who's coming, know what you're going to serve, know what entertainment you'll offer, have begun assembling ingredients and storable supplies, have ordered any tickets or made any special arrangements.

If you're having a birthday party and not making the cake yourself, order it from a bakery now. Also, start freezing trays of ice cubes. Store the cubes in the freezer in plastic freezer bags. But what you really must do now is roll up your sleeves and . . .

Clean!

Whatever location you've chosen for your party should be cleaned now, and cleaned very thoroughly. It may take some time if you're cleaning the basement or garage.

You'll need to sweep, vacuum, and dust. You'll have to wash windows, floors, and furniture. You might have to shake out curtains or slipcovers. It might be necessary to move boxes or plastic bags of stored items out of the way. Ask Mom or Dad where to put them.

If your party's going to be in the main part of the house, you should still be the one to give the room a good cleaning. When cleaning the living room or family room, move breakable and valuable things out of the way. Knickknacks, figurines, and delicate antique furniture should be safely tucked away where they can't be accidentally harmed.

TWO, FOUR, SIX, EIGHT, DECORATE!

No matter where you have the party, and no matter how simple it's going to be, you should decorate at least a little. Crepe paper streamers and balloons are traditional, and couldn't be easier to use. Don't be afraid to "play" with the crepe paper. It can be twisted and pleated or shredded or stretched. Wrap it around poles, crisscross it from beams, scallop it along the edge of your serving table. Instant celebration!

Lights

Tiny Christmas lights, especially white ones, work year-round for decorations. String them around windows and doorways, on large house plants, on bannisters and picture frames. Soften the regular lighting by replacing your usual bulbs with low-wattage ones (20 or 40 watt). Try pink bulbs.

Candles

Candles can create all sorts of moods, from eerie to cozy and romantic. Keep them away from drafts and flammable materials. Be sure that candles aren't too close to a wall or a ceiling. They can cause smoke damage. Unusual candle holders can be made from shiny red or green apples, cored and grouped in threes or fours. Cut off the bottoms of apples for stability.

Flowers

Fresh, dried, or paper flowers make every party place prettier. Keep arrangements simple: a pitcherful of tulips or daisies, or a mound of fresh green trimmings from an evergreen or shrub. Make centerpieces low so guests can see each other across the table.

P-DAY MINUS ONE

It's the final countdown. Get as much of this last-minute preparation done the afternoon and night before as you can, to save some rest time tomorrow. You can:

Decorate: String lights
Hang crepe paper streamers
Arrange furniture, candles, flowers
Note: Don't blow up balloons. They'll deflate.

Shop: Purchase any groceries you still need.

Cook: Almost anything can be cooked or baked now, and reheated tomorrow. Don't prepare anything that could get soggy, like Sloppy Joes.

Pick up: Dry cleaning or costume
Birthday cake
Film for camera
Candles

Cut up: Raw vegetables for dip (rinse well, dry, and store in refrigerator in plastic wrap)

Clean up: The kitchen when you're finished
The guest bathroom

Find: A safe, quiet place for your pets. Nothing can freak out a poor, innocent pet like being pawed at by a dozen high-spirited party animals.

The Best-Dressed Hostess

In all your activity on your guests' behalf, don't overlook someone else who deserves a little attention: yourself.

In order for you to have the most fun on party night, you have to feel great and look terrific. That means planning your outfit in advance, and there's no time like the present.

If you're planning on wearing something you already own, see if it needs mending, washing, or dry-cleaning. If you're planning to buy something new, schedule a shopping trip this weekend. That way, if you can't find what you're looking for, you have a whole week to figure out something else.

Keep in mind that you'll be serving things and moving around a lot. Plan on wearing comfortable shoes with low heels. Don't wear anything with loose, floppy sleeves. They're likely to get dragged through the food you're carrying, passing, or removing from the oven. Don't forget to plan the extras: jewelry, accessories, make-up, and hair.

> **TIP:** Costume parties are great fun because almost everyone likes dressing up. Costumes like this can usually be rented at a good price at a party store.

LET'S PARTY

The doorbell is ringing, and the first guest is here! Now the next one, and now another, and . . . it's party time.

Your guests will probably all arrive within ten minutes of each other, making a congested doorway and lots of commotion for a while. Ask one of the early arrivers to help you put away coats and direct people to the party area.

Then, after all that initial noise, something strange might happen: *dead silence*. It's weird, but true. Sometimes when a group of people—young or old, friends or strangers—find themselves in a planned social situation, they get very shy. Even the class clown can turn into a shrinking violet.

TIP: If silence breaks out, don't panic. Get some activity going. Pass the food. By all means, put on some music. Music helps fill in all those awkward silences. Who knows — a few people might even start dancing.

As you perform all your hostessing duties during the evening, those words—*don't panic*—should be remembered again and again. A good hostess does a lot more than serve food and introduce people, although those things certainly must be done. The really great hostesses have a good time at their own parties. They know that if the hostess is having fun and acting relaxed, the guests will take their cue and enjoy themselves too. However, if the hostess is frantically running around looking worried and hassled, the guests will find it harder to loosen up.

Have fun! Don't worry. No matter what happens, remember: you're among friends. Make sure anyone outside your regular crowd is introduced around and made to feel welcome. Make sure the refreshments are constantly replenished. Keep everyone busy. Don't let guests just sit around. There should be enough activities planned so nobody's bored or left out of it.

What To Do About Crashers

All right, your party is going along just beautifully. The food is delicious. Everyone has complimented you on the punch, the decorations, everything! You're having a wonderful time yourself.

Then you hear it: the sounds of engines revving and brakes squealing. Outside, radios are blaring and kids are yelling back and forth to each other. You look out the window and see four or five cars and a bunch of kids. You don't recognize any of them.

Party crashers are, unfortunately, a very common problem. It seems that when teenagers have a party, the word gets out. Sometimes it gets out as far as neighboring towns.

What should you do if a bunch of strangers want to crash your party? Well, first of all, don't just let it happen. Remember, you've been planning this affair for weeks. Why let someone spoil it? Besides, these kids may have liquor or drugs. On the other hand, you don't want to look like a jerk, either. You'd like to be able to handle the situation and still hold onto your cool.

At times like this you will be thankful that your parents are around. They might be outside already anyway, because of the noise. Avoid getting directly involved. Concentrate on your guests. Keep the music playing. Keep the refreshments coming, and let your parents take care of the problem. It's not a cop-out. It's one of the reasons your parents are there in the first place. You're only being responsible to your family and to the guests you *did* invite.

The Party's Over

All good things must end. One last dance, one last round of Trivial Pursuit, one last piece of cake or handful of chips, and that's it. Make sure that the ending time you and your parents have agreed on is honored. That may mean gently nudging your last few guests out the door. Just keep in mind that your parents are going to be a lot more willing to let you have another party if this one goes well. So play by the rules.

And now . . . the cleanup should begin. That gorgeous party room is a sorry sight. Melting ice cream, popped balloons, and crushed potato chips are all over the place. What a mess.

Well, it's not going to get cleaned up by just looking at it, so you might as well start. Arm yourself with a large plastic trash bag and throw anything disposable into it. Gather up plates, cups, or glasses that must be washed and bring them into the kitchen. Wipe up spills with damp paper towels. Put any returnable bottles into a separate bag. Refrigerate the food you're saving.

Then, after rinsing off plates, you might be able to go to bed. Of course, that depends on what agreement you've worked out with your parents. Chances are if you've done the initial cleanup tonight, your folks won't mind if you finish up tomorrow.

Do whatever you and your family have agreed. Once again, the better things work out this time, the easier it will be to persuade your folks to let you have another bash. Maybe an even bigger one!

BIBLIOGRAPHY

"A Crash Course in Party Confidence," by S. Bird, Seventeen. May 1988, pp. 174-5.

"Do-It-Yourself Spook House" [Halloween], National Geographic World. October 1988, pp. 19-23.

"Ho'-Made Makings" [Christmas Crafts], Teen. December 1988, p. 76.

"It's My Party," Seventeen. March 1988, pp. 264-7.

"Last-Minute Parties: The Best Kind," Glamour. January 1989, pp. 164-7.

"Party Lines: How To Banter With the Best," by J. C. Johnson, Mademoiselle. October 1988, p. 80.

"Slumber Party Pointers," Teen. May 1989, p. 49.

"Step-by-Step to a Dazzling Halloween Pumpkin," Redbook. October 1988, p. 16.

"Welcome to Party Paradise," Seventeen. May 1989, pp. 194-8.

"You Can Be a Party Animal — But You Can't Eat Like One," by E. Kunes, Mademoiselle. December 1988, pp. 136-7.

The Complete Book of Entertaining, by Elizabeth Post and Anthony Staffieri, Harper and Row, New York City, 1981.

Party or Holiday Sections of large cookbooks: The Joy of Cooking, Fannie Farmer Cookbook, Betty Crocker, etc.

INDEX